NORSE MYTHOLOGY

University Press
Copyright © 2019

Table of Contents

Editor's Note: Throughout this book, *italicized* text is quoted from translations of ancient literature. Summarized portions of stories from ancient poetic literature are placed in "quotations." Minor additions added to the text for clarification are placed in [brackets].

"*Full many a wonder is told us in stories old,
of heroes worthy of praise, of hardships dire,
of joy and feasting, of weeping and of wailing;
of the fighting of bold warriors; now ye may
hear wonders told.*"

From *Nibelungenlied;* Anonymous poet circa
1180-1210

Introduction

When we think of Norse mythology, we might think of armored breastplates and plaited beards in horned helmets, and we are naturally drawn to stories of fierce warriors and Viking raids. But Norse mythology is more than that. It is about the gods and goddesses who controlled the lives of men and women, their crops, their battles, and their fates. It is about the Nine Worlds of the Gods and Giants who began the world the Norsemen knew, and the poets and coders (writers) who documented that world for us.

Other than archaeological findings in the recent few decades - coupled with more recent technology such as DNA analysis, paleo-botany, and dendrochronology - much of what we know today about the day-to-day lives of famous Norsemen and women comes to us through the writings of one man, the 13th-century historian, poet, and politician, Snorri Sturluson. Author of the *Prose Edda* - a book of poems and prose that chronicles the lives of people like Eirik Thorvaldsson

(Eirik the Red), Beowulf, and other Germanic heroic legends - Sturluson also documented the history of the Norwegian warrior kings. He proposed that warriors who died in battle became gods, and that those gods often battled other gods or dead hero-kings.

Although he was born to a wealthy and influential family, Sturluson was raised among royalty in Iceland, an agreement made after his father was attacked while trying to settle a lawsuit. As compensation, Snorri was to be educated and raised by a Norwegian royal family. It was in this way that he was able to attend the best schools and make connections with people in positions of power.

He became a lawyer and was appointed law speaker of the Althing or Icelandic parliament. He also had a natural talent for poetry and writing. By royal invitation, he traveled to Norway, then Sweden, where he became well acquainted with the history of those countries, and as a house-guest of a jarl (chief), he wrote poetry about them.

However, poetic sagas are often prejudiced by the writer who may have found himself duty-bound to exaggerate the significance and magnitude of the deeds of family members or their political power.

While Norse mythology includes the tales and adventures of those who later became known as the Vikings, it begins with the religious and traditional ancestral stories that were handed down among generations, all of which revolved around the complex deities of the peoples of Iceland, Norway, Denmark, Finland, and Sweden.

They became known as heathens, a name coined because they lived in the "heaths", people who later converted to Christianity during the Middle Ages, but who fought against it and the onslaught of the English realm for hundreds of years. And like any broad religious narrative, their deities allowed them to make sense of the world they lived in; it gave meaning to their lives and strength in battle, among other things.

In *Song of the Valkyries*, for example, the writer describes a prophecy of the Battle of Clontarf in 1014 during which the warlord of Dublin goes up against the famous king Brian of Leinster. It is a solemn, menacing poem about joyless glory, terrifying slaughter, and a dreadful, blood-stained dawn.

According to the English translation, "*... a certain man saw twelve mailed and armed persons ride toward a hut, where they were lost to his sight. Edging close to the building, he peered through a chink and saw that strange and fearful women had set up a web, where the heads of men served as weights, and their entrails formed the woof and the weft, a sword acted as a weaver`s reed, and arrows as rods. They sang the* Song of the Valkyries, *before tearing the web down into pieces, and each one held a part in her hand. The women then mounted their horses and rode away – six to the south and six to the north. The battle maidens issued forth, mounted upon strident, fiery, wild horses, searching for souls of great warriors to carry away to the great halls of Valhalla.*"

Yet the history of the Norsemen and the gods and goddesses they believed in and built their world around never loses its capacity to captivate us. It is not dry history, but an often electrifying look at an innovative, highly religious, superstitious, and formidable culture.

Chapter 1

In the Beginning

Much of the mythology of ancient Greece and Rome, as well as Christianity, contains similar stories, with changes in names and places. The beginning of all modern religion starts with a Void where a god mysteriously appears out of that void and calls into existence a hierarchy of gods or rulers to oversee the deeds of men, who can, in some cases, aspire to become gods themselves through their deeds, or at the very least, to reach either 'heaven' or 'hell' by a similar path.

This is the outline of the Teutonic, pre-Christian religion that was embraced by the Old Norse culture. These are the doctrines, established by Odin among their ancestors, which are recorded in the Eddas of Iceland (*Icelandic Eddas*).

"In the beginning, before the heaven and the earth and the sea were created, the great abyss Ginungagap was without form and void, and the spirit of Fimbultyr moved upon the face of the deep, until the ice-cold rivers, the Elivogs, flowing from Niflheim [World of Fog; a wasteland of endless night]*, came in contact with the dazzling flames from Muspelheim* [Home of Destruction]*."*

This was before Chaos.

"And Fimbultyr said: Let the melted drops of vapor quicken into life, and the giant Ymer [Ymir; Confused Noise; the first Giant] *was born in the midst of Ginungagap."*

He was not a god, but the father of all the race of evil giants. This (he) was Chaos.

"And Fimbultyr said: Let Ymer be slain and let order be established. And straightway Odin and his brothers - the bright sons of Bure - gave Ymer a mortal wound, and from his body made they the universe; from his flesh, the earth; from his blood, the sea; from his bones, the rocks; from his hair, the trees; from his skull, the vaulted heavens; from his eye-brows, the bulwark called Midgard. And

the gods formed man and woman in their own image of two trees, and breathed into them the breath of life. Askr and Embla became living souls [the first two humans]*, and they received a garden in Midgard as a dwelling-place for themselves and their children until the end of time."* (From the *Poetic Edda*)

This was the Cosmos.

"The world's last day approaches. All bonds and fetters that bound the forces of heaven and earth together are severed, and the powers of good and of evil are brought together in an internecine feud. Loki advances with the Fenris-wolf and the Midgard-serpent, his own children, with all the hosts of the giants, and with Surt [fire god]*, who flings fire and flame over the world.*

This was the first war of the gods.

"Odin advances with all the asas and all the blessed einherjes. They meet, contend, and fall. The wolf swallows Odin, but Vidar, the Silent, sets his foot upon the monster's lower jaw, he seizes the other with his hand, and thus rends him till he dies. Frey encounters Surt, and terrible blows are given ere Frey

falls. Heimdal and Loki fight and kill each other, and so do Tyr and the wolf Garmr from the Gnipa Cave. Asa-Thor fells the Midgard-serpent with his Mjolnir, but he retreats only nine paces when he himself falls dead, suffocated by the serpent's venom. Then smoke wreathes up around the ash Yggdrasil, the high flames play against the heavens, the graves of the gods, of the giants, and of men are swallowed up by the sea, and the end has come.

This is Ragnarok, the twilight of the gods.

"But the radiant dawn follows the night. The earth, completely green, rises again from the sea, and where the mews have but just been rocking on restless waves, rich fields unplowed and unsown, now wave their golden harvests before the gentle breezes. The asas awake to a new life, Balder is with them again. Then comes the mighty Fimbultyr, the god who is from everlasting to everlasting; the god whom the Edda skald dared not name. The god of gods comes to the asas. He comes to the great judgment and gathers all the good into Gimle to dwell there forever, and evermore delights enjoy; but the perjurers and murderers and

adulterers he sends to Nastrand, that terrible hall, to be torn by Nidhug until they are purged from their wickedness."

This is Regeneration or the second coming of life on Earth.

Chapter 2

Niu Heimar: The Nine Worlds

The Nine Worlds or realms are depicted in three levels, with each being the home of various gods, magical creatures, and humans. The exact mapping is unclear, but Yggdrasil, the tree of life, stands in the middle with the three levels surrounding it. The Nine Worlds are Asgard, Midgard, Jotunheim, Vanaheim, Muspelheim, Niflheim, Alfheim, Svartalfheim, and Helheim.

The innermost world was Asgard, where the Aesir lived. Odin lived in Valhalla (Valhöll, "hall of the slain"), Thor lived in Trudheim, and Freyja lived in Folkvang. These were the great halls of Asgard believed by humans to be like the mansions of their own kings. They believed the only way to reach Asgard from Earth was by a bridge they called Bilfrost, which was actually a rainbow.

Beyond this inner realm was Midgard, where humans dwelled. It was believed to be located midway between Asgard and Utgard (synonymous with Jotunheim) or the outer place, the outer rim of Midgard, where giants lived with other elemental beings associated with untamed chaos. Between Utgard and Midgard was the sea.

Asgard
This is the Court of the Ás, home of the Æsir (gods) and Ásynjur (goddesses), ruled by Odin, and which contains all the halls of the gods including Gimli, the hall of the righteous and Valhalla, the hall of the slain.

Jotunheim
Jotunnheimar is the freezing land of the Jotun or giants. Some references suggest that Jotuns lived on the perimeter of Midgard, outside of the realm of humans. Others suggest it was one realm, just like Asgard, with many dwelling places.

Neiflheim
The underworld or lowest place on the tree filled with poisoned water. Here is where the icy rivers (elivagir) poured into Ginungagap and froze. When the fire god, Surt, melted the

ice, it turned to mist, which released the first giant, Ymir.

Midgard

Halfway between Asgard and Neiflheim, home of humans and dark, dark elves (Dökkálfr), Midgard is connected to Asgard by the rainbow bridge, Bifrost, and is the path for the slain to get to Valhalla. It is surrounded by water, wherein lives the Midgard Serpent. It is here that the gods created the first humans from tree trunks, Askr (Ask), a male, and Embla, a female.

Vanaheim

Home of the Vanir, gods of earth, fertility, and abundance.

Muspelheim

The realm of fire and the home of Destruction; ruled over by Surt, the fire giant; a realm of Helheim.

Álfheim

Álfheimr; also referred to as Ljósálfheimr; home of the fair elves or light elves (Ljósálfr).

Svartálfheim

Svartálfheimr; sometimes referred to as Niôavellir; home of dwarves.

Helheim
Hel; Helheimr; home of the dishonored dead; a realm pushed deep into the cosmos by the gods so humans would not have to suffer its freezing cold.

Yggdrasil: The Tree of Life
Yggdrasil is depicted as an eternal green ash tree that extends to the heavens, with three enormous, long deep roots and branches that stretch out over all the Nine Worlds. The first of the three roots goes to Asgard, the home of the gods (Æsir and Vanir) and the light elves; the second goes to Midgard (Middle Earth) the land of the giants (Jotuns), humans and dark elves; the third goes to Niflheim (Hel), world of the dead where the dragon, Nidhug, gnaws on the root and sucks the blood from the dead bodies and where the Queen Hel presided over the fire god.

At the top of Yggdrasil lives the eagle, which represents both strength and death and is one of the three birds of Odin. The eagle is the bitter enemy of the dragon, Niflheim (sometimes called Nithog).

Running up and down the tree is the squirrel, Ratatosk, who does what he can to antagonize them against each other. This symbol may represent man's struggle between good and evil or the constant battle between good and evil to rule over man.

The First War of the Gods

In the beginning, each god had his or her special gift. They lived in harmony in the golden era when the world was without malice. The Æsir, the gods and goddesses of war, and the Vanir, the fertility gods, played in the meadows together, listening and talking and enjoying the blessings of the Tree of Life, Yggdrasil.

"One day the seer and enchantress, Gullveig, came to Odin with talk of gold, for this was what she lusted after, and the Æsir speared her for her greed, for they loathed such things. They burned her and she emerged unscathed from the fire; thrice did they burn her, yet she lived, and the Vanir swore vengeance against the Æsir. And so, the war between the gods began."

"Asgard and Vanaheim were battle-raged, but each was equal to the other, and so an exchange was made in truce that Freyr and Freyja of the Vanir should live in Asgard, and Hoenir and Mimir of Vanaheim should go to live with the Vanir. Thusly was the golden age of the gods ended."

Ragnarök

Ragnarök is the end of the world, the day of doom for gods and humans, the final battle between the Aesir and Jotuns. It was believed that a deadly frost would cover the land, and all living things would perish. The sun would be blackened, and the end of the world would begin.

"The Fimbulwinter will cause a three-year frost to cover the land, upon which all vegetation and animals will die from the bitter cold. The sun will be covered with gray clouds as thick as the sheep's wool, and the all-knower will warn the giants that Ragnarok has begun; then will be warned the gods and all the dead."

"Brothers will kill brothers; a horn will sound loudly, the warning from Heimdall will blow, and this will be the battle at the end, the day

that all the Vikings will pick up their swords and armor to fight side by side with the Aesir."

"The giant, Surt, will set the world on fire and the mighty Midgard serpent will emerge from the sea and engulf the Vigrid plains, spraying poison and causing destruction."

"The sun and moon will be swallowed by wolves, and Yggdrasil will fall to the ground. Odin, too, will be killed by the Wolf, and Thor and the Serpent will kill each other. Finally, an inferno will cause the world to sink into a boiling sea."

"And then shall a new world rise from the sea, shimmering with green and gold, and the two who were left behind in the battle, the man and the woman who found sheltering in the sacred tree, will emerge and repopulate the land. Modi and Magni will inherit the hammer of Thor, their father; Vidar and Vali and Honir will sit in the throne of Odin, their father; and in Idavoll they will build a new house with a roof of gold, for they are the only gods now."

"And there will be a new place called Okolnir where it will never be cold though it is in the *mountains of Nidafjoll. And the shore of corpses that greets the screaming north wind shall have walls made of writhing snakes and a pit for thieves and murderers who will be the food of Nidhug, the great dragon."*

Chapter 3

The Gods of Valhalla

Like many early civilizations, the Scandinavians believed in many gods, and the cosmological world was conceived as a flat circle that was divided into three distinct regions that shared a common center.

There are hundreds of gods and demigods in Norse mythology, and they were believed to have been mortal, just like humans. They could be captured, killed or tricked, and hoped they would live long enough to see Ragnarok.

Odin

Odin is described in the *Poetic Edda* and the *Prose Edda* as "*the highest and oldest of the gods.*" This is the Norse god of war and poets - the father of the battle-slain. His role was to inspire great oratory and to give fighting men courage in battle. He ruled over poets and warriors and watched the entire world from high atop Yggdrasil in Valhalla. The word *valr* means "the slain" or "those slain in battle."

"He rules all things, and however powerful the other gods are, they all serve him as children serve their father. Odin is called All-father because he is the father of all the gods; he is also called Valfather because his chosen sons are all those who die in battle. Valhöll is for them."

Odin was the "god of the hanged," also called the "helmeted one." In the second part of Snorri Sturluson's *Prose Edda*, the *Skáldskaparmál* or language of poetry, he describes in "poesy" a dialog between Ægir, god of the sea, and Bragi, god of poetry:

"Now I will tell men the virtue of the terrible Jarl;
Allfather's song-surf streams;
Now is the flight of eagles over the field;
The sailors of the sea horses hie them to the Hanged-God's gifts and feasting
With the Hanged-God's helmet the hosts have ceased from going by the brink;
Not pleasant the bravest held the venture
Oft the Gracious One came to me at the holy cup of the Raven-God

The king of the stem-plowed sea's gold from the skald in death sundered."

Odin had two pet ravens, Huginn (Thought) and Muninn (Memory), which embodied his function as the god of wisdom.

Numerous prophesies in the Eddas tell us that the monstrous gray wolf, Fenrir, who is destined to be the death of Odin, will feature prominently in the last battle of the gods and men against monsters and giants – the Battle of Ragnarok.

"And Odin, with his eagle and his helmet and his spear in hand, will ride Sleipnir with the enormous army of Asgard and will go with all the gods and brave einherjar [battle slain] *to the battleground."*

Thor

A son of Odin, he is responsible for natural phenomena such as wind, rain, thunder, and lightning, and ruled over farmers and the common man. He is associated with oak trees and is often remembered for his famous magical hammer, belt, and iron gloves.

Thor is believed by some to be the most powerful of the gods, and he appears in the *Prose Edda* predominantly in a protective role. An idiosyncrasy of Thor is that he is vulnerable without his hammer. People wore amulets or pendants in the shape of Thor's hammer because they believed this would invoke his protection.

"I am the god of War, the Thunderer in the Northland, my fortress, and I will reign forever; here amid the icebergs, I will rule the nations. Miölner the Mighty is my hammer, and there is none among the Jotuns and sorcerers who can withstand it. I hurl it far off and it returns to me, redoubling my strength."

"The light of the heavens, in flashes of crimson, you may behold, and it is I, Thor, with my red beard blown by the night wind, affrighting the land. My eyes are lightening and the wheels of my chariot are thunder. My hammer rings in the earthquake!"

"For it is by force that the world is ruled, and strength alone is triumphant. This is Thor's-Day! Thou art a god, too, and thus single-handed unto the combat, gauntlet here, I defy thee!"

Baldur

Also son of Odin, Baldur was the god of the summer sun, said to be so bright that light shone from him. His mother was the goddess Frigg who had a dream that foretold of his death, and through the trickery of Loki, Baldur was indeed killed by a spear made of mistletoe.

"Most beloved Baldur, most joyful, who makes the gladdened heart, my dreams have been ominous for your grave misfortune."

Odin consulted with the seeress, and when he returned to Frigg, he told her of the prophecy, so she secured the oaths of all living things that her son should not be harmed. But Loki, the trickster, saw an opportunity for mischief. He realized that the mistletoe was the only living thing that had not yet sworn its oath.

"And so it was that Loki tricked the blind Hodr to throw the shaft of mistletoe which killed the joyful god [Baldur]."

Freyja

Freyja is the goddess of love and fertility, and the embodiment of female sexual power, a sorceress who is skilled at *seiðr* (say-der), meaning "snare." This type of magic is particular to Norse mythology and gave the ability to change the course of destiny set forth by the three Norns.

"*She entered into the prophetic place, where all thought is fluid, and roamed the Nine Worlds, traveling in spirit, seeking to change the curse on the Hard One for she saw his end in Stamford Bridge. And in the secret mind, where there were luck and healing for the sick, control over the storms of Thor and calling for the food of the forest, there could be found no false future for Hardrada. He would be first maimed in his manhood, his men pushed back by the enemy, and the battle lost in the river, with head split asunder, and the blood of his family spewed across the plain.*"

Freyr

He is the brother of Freyja and the god of male potency, good weather, good harvests, and fertile beasts; he is the son of the sea god, Njörd.

"In Ragnarok did Freyr fight the fire-giant, Surt, with a stag's antler, for he was without his magic sword which he had given to Skimir, his shield-bearer. He was the first to be slain at the end of the world, yet he was the bright slayer of Beli, the giant; he was Beli's bright slayer."

Loki the Trickster

He is the blood brother of Odin and the son of giants who was adopted into the family of the Aesir, and who brought trouble everywhere he went. He is a mischief-maker and the god of wildfire. He is evil at heart, cunning, and without loyalty. He is also a shapeshifter who might appear in the form of a water creature, human, insect, or animal, and he is the cause of the death of the god, Baldur.

"Loki came from the giants and was unlike the other gods, for he seeks only to cause mischief among gods and men. He looks for trouble and redoubles it in trickery. Now he is evil and wears the blood of Baldur; by the troll, woman is his offspring, the wolf Fenrir, and the serpent of Midgard and Hel, the goddess of death."

Aegir

Aegir is Lord of the Sea and one of the three Jotuns who lived in Asgard. He predates the Aesir and Vanir and lives in the coral caves under the sea. He is the brother of the wind and fire.

"*A great feast was in his hall, Brime, where the drinking horns filled themselves by his magic and all the gods did eat of his bounty. In Aegir's hall they ate from the shifting sand and the watery billows and glassy brine; from pearl shells they ate sea flowers and dew; the tides were above and below but the winds and waves were absent.*"

Hel

She is the daughter of Loki who became queen of the underworld known as Niflheim. She rules over illness and the sickbed, old age, misfortune, hunger and starvation. At the gates of Hel stands Garmr, the Hel Hound, who will signal any new arrivals, and the dragon Nidhug will then suck their blood so they may easily join the army of the dead. When Ragnarok arrives, the end of the world, this army will attack the humans in Midgard.

"*From the high hall of Hel were raised the wolf Fenrir and the serpent Jormungandr, and the prophecies spoke of their disasters, so that Odin called for them and threw the serpent into that deep sea that lies round all lands.*"

From there, Hel visited Baldur in a dream and told him that in three days' time, she would "clasp him in her arms."

"And so it was that in three days, the mistletoe which caused his wound would bring his end."

Chapter 4

Helpers and Spirits

There was an abundance of minor deities that Norseman looked to for everything from peace and justice to friendship and building materials.

Valkyries

The Valkyrie in Norse mythology are the daughters of Odin, and they appear continually throughout the Icelandic sagas, in the *Poetic Edda*, and in runic inscriptions. There seems to be an undefined number, with many names appearing in the poems.

These female supernatural creatures are associated with fate. They choose those who will be slain in battle and then escort them to Valhalla, home of the gods, ruled by Odin. They also appear in the text as the lovers of heroes and other fictitious mortals, and may be accompanied by ravens, swans, or horses.

They are called wish maidens, choosers of the slain, maids, and wish fulfillers and are often conflated with other spirits: Norns who spin the threads of life, and Dísir, the guardians of individuals.

"The great King Haakon made his final request as he lay on the battlefield, that, dying among the heathens, he should be given a burial place as seems most fitting. And so he died on the same rock upon which he was born and was greatly mourned. His finest clothing and armor were laid with him and the words were spoken according to the custom of heathen men, and so he went on his way to Valhalla."

"For who should be chosen among those in battle to dwell with Odin in Valhalla? Those who see Göndul leaning on her spear shaft or sitting gratified on horseback are goodly bidden home, for they are worthy for the gods to grant it and they shall ride forth to the green homes of the godheads."

Norns
There are three Norns whose names are Past, Present, and Future, and they are also

goddesses who spin the threads of life and decide the fates of men. They are responsible for bringing water to the Yggdrasil, the Tree of Life at the center of the world.

"And so to respect the goddesses and gain favor for the child, porridge was given to the newborn babe, that he might have long life, good health, and prosperity."

Jotuns

Jotuns are giants with superhuman strength and were considered to be the first living beings.

"Ymir, the first of the living, was the origin of the world, and his home was Jotunheim of the Nine Worlds, where he ate of the fish from the rivers and streams, and from the forests, he took the animals for food, for the land was not yet fertile."

It may be difficult to understand a strong faith that revolves around this type of thinking, but, even among Christians, Nordic beliefs in elves, trolls, and nature spirits have been handed down from generation to generation.

The Asatru Association was formed in Reykjavik in 1972 and received recognition from the Icelandic government as an official religious organization. In 2012, construction began on the first temple in more than 1,000 years to honor the ancient Norse gods. At the cost of nearly $1 million, the 4,000 square foot temple will exist in harmony with the natural rock of the hillside and is expected to be completed by the end of 2019.

Admittedly, the ceremonies and rituals of the Asatru Association "do not read the medieval texts literally and eschew a strict interpretation of Norse mythology for its more spiritual qualities." Instead, they view the ancient text as a poetic metaphor for human nature. It seems that some people love the appeal of their Viking roots and "really want to go back to the Viking era."

Chapter 5

Creatures of Magic

The Medieval Age was replete with its share of fascinating mythical creatures that influenced the daily lives of people. They were mischievous, dangerous and magical, and each had their place in Viking lore.

Dwarves

Dwarves were believed to be created from the maggots living inside the bodies of giants.

Dain the Dwarf made the cursed sword that must slay a man before it can be returned to its sheath. Anyone hit with this sword would die or suffer a wound that would never heal.

Fafnir the Dwarf is the son of the dwarf king magician, Hreidmar, and is the guard of his father's house.

"One day, Loki was traveling with Odin, and Hreidmar captured them. Loki was forced to turn over a ransom of red gold, and Fafnir killed his father to get the gold for himself. His greed grew so great that he became a gold hoarding dragon, whom Sigurd heard of. Sigurd made his way to the house of Hreidmar to obtain the treasure, but a dragon had taken it, which was Fafnir, and it was stored in the lair of the beast. Fafnir warned Sigurd that any man who should steal the treasure would die, but Sigurd knew it was the destiny of man to live ambitiously and that he would die someday anyway. To this end, he killed Fafnir the Dwarf/Dragon, seized the gold, and ate the heart of the dwarf."

Hit the Ogre

Hítardalur was a big farm and ancient church in Mýrasýslu in the Hitardalur valley. Legend says that the ogre, Hit, and a half human-half ogre named Barour Snadrellsás were traveling through the mountains returning to their lair, which they must reach before daybreak or they would be turned to stone. They missed their timing and were indeed turned into a pair of peculiar rock formations still found to be in that place.

Elves

Light elves were what we might call guardian angels. They are minor gods of nature and have the power to help humans without actually interfering in their lives. They cannot change the course of fate, but they are magical and can inspire humans.

"The white *älvor* appeared by the grace of the god Freyr, clad in silk, and the Dane was raped by her beauty, he that slew in battle all who would come before him with the wielding of his great ax. Yet Eirik fell beneath the elf, and they drank together, that he might be inspired in battle."

Dark elves live to annoy humans and make trouble for them. They, too, are magical and are described as being "hideous."

"And so in the night, the dark elf sat upon Ragnar's chest as he slept, and the warrior dreamed of the battle ahead. When he woke, though the sun had not yet risen, dread filled him, yet he knew not why, for his men were readied with armor and supplies and outnumbered the coming forces. He mounted his steed, who reared up as though frightened, and the mist that was *dökkálfar*, the black elf, passed before his eyes."

Cats

Cats were feared and thought to be witches in disguise. The goddess Freya, who is a sorceress, had her chariot pulled by two enormous cats.

"The great forest cats were wild, yet Freya tamed them by her magic to pull her cart, and the *skagcatts* loved her, for she was kind to them and gave those two fish and mead."

Dragons

Dragons were thought to be magical, and there are many in Viking mythology, including Nidhoggr, aka Dread Biter, who lived at the foot of Yggdrasil; the Firedrake of Beowulf fame; Jormundandr the Midgard Serpent; and Fafnir, the dwarf son of magician Hreidman, who killed his father and was turned into a dragon by his greed.

"The dragon sat at the bubbling cauldron that was Niflheim, at the source of the rivers of the world, and devoured the corpses of the evil-doers, enjoying the taste of the dead, for Nidhoggr was evil itself and destined to survive Ragnarok, the doom."

Eagles

To the Norse, the eagle is a symbol of strength and death.

"And the walls of Valhalla were guarded by wolves and eagles, and in it I saw my place among my people, shields and spears in hand, ready to stand with Odin at Ragnarok, for that land is hallowed, lying near gods and elves, and the glorious eagles."

Wights

These were creatures believed to protect homes, farms, and villages. They were spirits with no particular form but were thought to be more like elves than humans, and could be seen only in the right light.

"The *landvætir* were agitated by the pole which Egil set up so that they would go astray, wanting these guardians to confound the king and queen out of the country. And so the spirits went out to the west and north, to the hillsides and hollows, large and small, until the spirits lived there no more and the earth around became a wasteland."

Ravens

These are the symbol of Odin. His two ravens were named Huginn (Thought) and Muninn (mind or memory).

"The birds flew with a message to Odin, from Midgard they came with news for the raven god, for the birds can speak by the magic of Odin. Each day they set forth to fly and each day Odin mourned for their loss that they may not return. 'For Huginn I fear, lest he come not home, but for Muninn my care is more. For Huginn is for the hanged, yet Muginn is for the slain in battle who will join me in the halls of Valhalla.'"

Wolves

Fenrir, Fenrisulfr, Vanagandr, and Hrodvitnir were all names for the famed wolf who would be the undoing of Odin at Ragnarok.

"The beast, the monstrous wolf, the second sorrow, whom I came to strike down and slaughter with my hands and drive through with my sword, into the heart of him, yet the prophecy will stand and he will be my undoing in the final battle. Side by side with Beli's bright slayer will I fight Vanagandr, then shall sweet Frigg fall."

Chapter 6

The Age of the Vikings

"Better it is to die in battle with honor than to live in shame because you did not defend your people." Bjarnar Saga, *Hítdælakappa*

A book on Norse mythology would not be complete without some mention of those men who came to be called Vikings, who they were and what they did.

The Skaldic and Eddic poetry or sagas, which tell us about Viking and Norse history, were written almost 300 years after the end of what is referred to as the Viking Age. In many cases, stories and legends were embellished to edify the feats of ancestors. But some of their stories comes to us through Viking runes or ancient Germanic marks that were meant to have some significance regarding a particular event, place, or person.

It is difficult at best to discern fact from fable, truth from legend, and to what degree a tale has been embellished or exaggerated. Added to this is modern media's version of history as told through television and film, including *The Hobbit* and *Lord of the Rings* trilogy, writings which were inspired by Norse mythology.

The Viking Age began in the year 793 and lasted about 300 years.

In pre-Christian, North-Germanic clan culture in Scandinavia, people were obligated to take revenge for the deaths or injury of their loved ones by others, regardless of the reason.

The Roman Empire had disappeared, and the three major empires were now the Byzantine in the east, the Franks to the south, and the Muslims south of the Frankish Empire. Their expansion pushed trade routes northward, creating ideal conditions for piracy. Scandinavian tribes were growing into dynasties, and this more centralized power often led to conflict among tribes. But none of this accounted for the rage for which Viking warriors were renowned.

In fact, it was an affront by Charlemagne, then King Charles or Charles the Great, whose mission as king was to expand Christianity. After conquering the Muslims, Arabs, Spanish, Lombards, and Slavs, he reached north to lower Scandinavia. It was there that he destroyed the sacred Irmensul, the Saxons' holy shrine, and it is believed that this was the turning point that triggered Norse revenge. Charlemagne invaded their lands and destroyed religious sanctuaries, he burned cultural institutions, and exiled anyone who did not accept Christianity.

In retaliation, Norsemen made the first major raid of note on Lindisfarne in 793, a monastery off the coast of northeast England, which housed an elaborate wealth of artifacts and decoration.

According to reports at the time in the *Anglo-Saxon Chronicle*, the weather condition during the raid on Lindesfarne was one of "high winds and lightning flashes" which would be interpreted today as stormy and with poor visibility. In this way, the Vikings were able to gain closer access without being seen.

They continued to burn Christian churches and monasteries. In another account, a 12th-century English chronicler writes:

"In the same year, the pagans from the northern regions came with a naval force to Britain like stinging hornets and spread on all sides like fearful wolves, robbed, tore and slaughtered not only beasts of burden, sheep, and oxen, but even priests and deacons, and companies of monks and nuns."

But these men were not organized in a military defense; they were simply chieftain-led tribes from Denmark, Norway, and Sweden who generally fought against each other. Now they began to unite over a common bond. They were much more than a group of men who stepped on shore and burned down a few churches. They set out in a rage of indifference, setting in place a type of psychological terror that preceded their arrival on any shore. When their boats were seen in the distance, people literally "ran for the hills," and trained soldiers trembled.

"From the tips of his toes to his neck, each man is tattooed dark green with designs, with eye markings that made him appear exotic, disconcerting or alarming, and they contorted their faces into grotesque and frightening masks. They display no empathy for their victims and show extreme violence and savagery on the battlefield."

The Sagas talk about men called berserkers, a term used for a few distinct warriors who "fought naked or scantily clad, deliberately inducing themselves into a battle frenzy which seemed to transform them into extraordinary beings beyond the ken of most, having superhuman strength which allowed them to feel no pain in their delirium."

Those who chose to enter the battlefield would suffer unimaginable blows in defense of his fellows so that he might enter Valhalla. Here is a brutal example of the type of atrocity these men inflicted and withstood in battle:

"They caused the bloody eagle to be carved on the back of Ælla, and they cut away all the ribs from the spine and ripped out his lungs...and that was [also] *Halfdan's death."*

The "bloody eagle" is a reference to the way an opponent might be cut up. They would open his back, cut out the ribs, and open his lungs, so they looked like wings, thus emulating the shape of the eagle.

They deliberately drowned monks as if to demonstrate some travesty of baptism, and blasphemed holy altars and treasures.

"They cut up Bible clasps and crosses and reshaped them into items of personal ornamentation" in what was apparently an overt display of cultural disrespect.

Thus it was that the pagans, or heathens, those men who went "viking" or plundering, who were referred to in terms of their religion, became *flotman, saeman, sceigdman*, or *aescman* – all terms for seaborne raiders - would eventually be known as Vikings.

Chapter 7

Viking Heroes and Legends

"Lo, there do I see my father; Lo, there do I see my mother and my brothers and my sisters. Lo, there do I see the line of my people back to the beginning. Lo, they do call to me; they bid me take my place among them in the halls of Valhalla where thine enemies have been vanquished; where the brave shall live forever. Nor shall we mourn, but rejoice for those that have died the glorious death."

A hero or legend in Viking lore might not always be a "good guy" in the way we think of legendary heroes today. Generally, the fiercer they were, the more the writers and poets turned them into heroes and documented their deeds.

A *saga*, which simply means *story*, was written as a historical document, more or less, and could have been handed down by word of mouth through generations, or could be a wholly artistic creation. Long, epic poems were written in a grand style that exemplified individuals, and both sagas and epics were generally written many years after the end of the Viking Age.

There were sagas of the Scandinavian kings, sagas of the Greenlanders, and Chivalric sagas, among other types. The Icelandic sagas, praising the heroic deeds of members of Icelandic families, are considered to be the highest form of classical saga writing. However, the more accurate writings might be those classified as contemporary sagas, which were written in the period, soon after the actual events occurred.

Then there are the legendary sagas that blend history with myth and paint a picture that is both entertaining and insightful regarding how these people viewed their heroes.

Epic poems are extensive narratives about a historical event, but they may not necessarily be factual. They were often oratory and were handed down by memory, so they changed in the telling over the generations.

Beowulf

One of the most famous and cherished of these stories for modern historians is *Beowulf*, the oldest surviving Anglo-Saxon epic poem written in the Old English. The surviving copy is believed to be from circa 1000 and was discovered in England in the 1600s. However, the original was probably composed somewhere between 700 and 950.

Although it is written in the language used by the Anglo-Saxons between 450 and 600, and the story is about the adventures of a pagan, based on references in the text, it was likely written by a monk or court poet with Christian beliefs.

It incorporates components of Anglo-Saxon tradition with Christian moral principles in an extraordinary look at the journey of one man. *Beowulf* emphasizes values that were important to Norse warriors, such as courage, loyalty to one's comrades, and honor for those who fight and die bravely among those for whom fighting was a way of life. It reflects the warrior culture of ancient Germanic peoples.

Beowulf tells us about a Norse warrior who possessed the strength of 30 men. He rescued Denmark and Sweden from monsters that were terrorizing the people of that land, particularly a monster named Grendel, who lurked in the dark swamps of Hrothgar's kingdom.

"Grendel attacked the great hall at night, when the warriors were quieted by drink and much merriment and tales of their victories in battle. In the morning, Hrothgar was assailed with the blood and remains of Grendel's attack and sent up his cries to the heavens."

The next night, Grendel returns and kills again. For twelve long years, he came killing warriors and farmers, women, and children, and still the attacks did not cease. Prayers for protection did not help, and eventually, the great hall was abandoned.

The stories of Grendel's horror went out to kingdoms far and wide, where they reached the land of a man named Beowulf, one who was renowned for killing great sea monsters and giants in the hills and caves of Sweden. His skill and courage in battle caused him to be thought of as a hero of the people, so he sailed to Denmark to rid them of the monster, Grendel.

"Fourteen brave men did he take on his ship, and at Heorot he was much welcomed by Hrothgar. A great feast was prepared in his honor, yet one named Unferth did not believe the tales of his bravery. 'Had you been as brave as you believe yourself to be, Unferth, Grendel would no longer be terrorizing the land.' In this, the king was confident that Grendel would finally be defeated by Beowulf."

"And so it was that Grendel appeared that night and engaged in a battle with Beowulf, who seized the monster by the arm and ripped it from his powerful body, and he returned to his cave to die. But the struggle was not over, for Grendel's mother vowed revenge."

Beowulf and several warriors track the monster to her lair in the swamps, but she is invulnerable to the swords and weapons of men. A struggle ensues, and Beowulf is dragged through the gory swamp to her cave, where he sees a mighty sword hanging from a wall.

"He grabbed the sword and with one monumental blow cut off the monster's head. He cut off the head of Grendel's corpse which lay behind its mother, and Beowulf carried the two through the swamp along with the melted remains of the mighty sword that slew the monster. And so he was awarded *wergild* for his bravery and returned with his men to Sweden to become their king."

The practice of offering *wergild* was traditional in early Germanic societies. This was the price set on a person's life based on their value to society. In the event of death, particularly on the battlefield, that person's family would receive *wergild*, and this custom replaced the practice of seeking revenge for the loss of a loved one.

In the second half of this epic poem, even though he is now an old man, Beowulf goes on to slay a dragon that is terrorizing his own kingdom.

"The great dragon slept on an ancient treasure, and when Beowulf's slave came upon it, he thought to steal a golden cup to please his king. But the dragon was cunning and counted his treasure each day, for he was greedy and quick to notice the missing cup. So he flew into the countryside, breathing fire and destroying all the homes in the villages."

"And Beowulf took with him to the dragon's lair eleven warriors of great repute, whereby they might slay the beast. But the king entered alone for the sake of his men, and in the battle, was fatally wounded, though the dragon was also killed."

"The great warrior and king, Beowulf, was burned on a cliff overlooking the sea, and the ancient treasure which was locked in the dragon's lair and was burned with him in the ceremony to praise him."

Here is a look at some of the prominent Viking heroes, legends, and bad guys:

Ragnar Lodbrok: Ragnar Hairy Breeches (circa 745-794)

Known as Ragnar Hairy Breeches, Ragnarr Loðbrók was a Norse king, considered to be a hero. He was the curse of France and England and the father of Ivar the Boneless, Bjorn Ironside, Halfdan Ironside, Halfdan

Ragnarsson, Ubba, and Sigurd Snake-in-the-Eye.

According to legend, Ragnar distinguished himself by many raids and conquests, particularly in the first siege of Paris, until he was eventually seized by his foe, King Ælla of Northumbria and killed by being thrown into a pit of snakes. His sons, Halfdan Ragnarsson and Ivar the Boneless, bloodily avenged him by invading England with the Great Heathen Army in what would ultimately be a fourteen-year war.

Ivar Ragnarsson: Ivar the Boneless (794-873)

Ivar Ragnarsson, aka Ivar the Boneless, was a son of Ragnar Lodbrok, a Viking warlord of exceptional ferocity and cruelty, and reputed to be a berserker. The Sagas describe him thusly:

"*Only cartilage was where bone should have been.*"

Perhaps this was not a literal description, but a way of saying he was extremely flexible. He was reported to be very large, dwarfing other men, with powerful arms able to carry a bow that was much stronger and with heavier arrows.

In 873, the Great Viking Army of Ivar Ragnarsson is reported to have wintered in Repton, England, and the *Saga of Ragnar Lodbrok*, Ivar's father, states that Ivar the Boneless was buried in England. During an excavation at the churchyard of St. Wystan's in Repton in Derbyshire, the skeleton of a 9-foot tall Viking warrior was uncovered, and archeologists believe it to be the remains of Ivar the Boneless.

Harald Halfdanarson: Harald I, Harald Fair-Hair (858-942)

Haraldr Halfdanarson is the tyrant son of Halfdan the Black, and as a boy, he became king after Halfdan's death. Known as Harald Fair-Hair, he was the person who consolidated the territories of Norway into a unified country, making him the official founder of Norway.

"His hair grew thick with a magnificent sheen very much like silk, and he was the handsomest of men, very strong and big of build." He took an oath not to cut, trim, or even comb his hair or beard until he became king, and so until then, he was known as Shock-Head or Tangle-Hair.

One of his sons was Erik Blood-Axe, and another was Hakon the Good, who both became kings after his death.

Thorfinn Torf-Einarsson: Thorfinn Skull-Splitter (890-963)

Thorfinn Torf-Einarsson was Earl of Orkney in the 10th century and appears briefly in *St. Olaf's Saga.* He joined with Erik Blood-Axe in a raid in England, and later, the earldom was weakened by murder plotted among the ranks of the family. The unstable reigns of each successive earl generally ended in violence caused by dynastic infighting.

Egil Skallagrimmson (904-995)

Egil's Saga touts this person to be the greatest Viking bard, a man who was a fierce warrior but who was also gifted with the art of making poetry. Unfortunately, he killed the son of Erik Blood-Axe and was sentenced to death. However, because he was able to recite an exceptionally fine poem to King Erik, he was spared execution.

"I dragged my oak ship to sea and loaded my vessel's hold with its cargo of praise, for the great King Erik who escaped the arrow's weaving while other men sank to the ground. In this, Erik won his glorious name."

In another poem, he writes:

"I have been with sword and spear, slippery with bright blood where kites are wheeled. And how well we violent Vikings clashed while red flames gorged men's roofs and we, raging, killed and killed."

"Now things go hard with me. On the headland stands the sister of Odin's enemy, yet serene, in good heart and undismayed, I shall meet death face to face."

Erik Haraldsson: Erik Blood-Axe (910-954)

Erik Haraldsson became known as Blood-Axe because of his savage feuding, horrific even by Viking standards, and for the murder of four of his brothers in a bid for his father's throne. He was then usurped as king by his youngest brother, Hakon the Good, and was exiled to England, where he became King of York for a time until he was killed in battle. He was the last Viking king of Northumbria, and his death marked the final step toward a united England. His funeral ode describes the preparations for the arrival of King Erik in Valhalla:

"What dream was that, said Odin, when I thought before dawn I was making Valhalla ready for a slaughtered army? I roused my great champions, bade the Valkyries wake, strew the benches, washed out the beer mugs, and brought out wine for a prince who is coming from the world. I await such noble fighting men as will make my heart rejoice."

Harald Gormsson: Harald Blue-Tooth (935-985)

Harald Gormsson was the son of King Gorm the Old and ruled as king of Denmark from around 958 and king of Norway around 970. He is believed to have been forcibly removed from this throne by his son, Swein Fork-Beard. The appellation Blue-Tooth is somewhat of a mystery. Some say he had one bad tooth, which was dark in color. Others say he wore only blue garments, which used an expensive dye to emphasize his royal status.

An inscription on a large stone in Jelling, Denmark (referred to as the Jelling stone, of which there were several) states that Harald turned the Danes to Christianity, and he is also credited with building the oldest known bridge in Scandinavia, the Ravninge Bridge.

Erik Thorvaldsson: Erik the Red-Beard (950-1002)

Erik Thorvaldsson was nicknamed Erik the Red for his red hair and beard. He was a principal player in the Viking colonization of Greenland. Once banished from Iceland, he spent three years in exile, with much of that time being spent exploring the long coastline. When he returned with tales of the land he discovered, he called it Green Land so it would be more attractive to settlers. However, most of this island was wilderness made of rock and ice. With a colony of 25 ships that set sail in the summer of 985, only 14 of them arrived in the new land.

Two settlements were created, one on the eastern shore and one on the western, about 300 miles apart in what is now Qaqortoq and Vestribyggo, and Erik was the chieftain of Greenland where he became respected and wealthy. As the population grew, an infectious disease took the lives of many, including Erik.

Sveinn Tjuguskegg: Sweyn I, Swein Fork-Beard (954-1014)

Sveinn Tjuguskegg, aka Sweyn I Fork-Beard, was another king of Denmark, England, and parts of Norway. He was the son of Harald Blue-Tooth and the father of Cnut the Great, who led a rebellion against his father, deposing him and driving him out. Because his father had converted to Christianity, he was given the Christian name Otto. However, he never used that name, though he may be referred to as Otto in some literature.

There are various accounts of his deeds. Some say he was a persecutor of Christians and others say he was ordering churches to be built in Denmark throughout a 14-year alleged exile, while at the same time leading raids against England.

One thing historians agree on is that he led numerous raids in his effort to conquer England between 1002 and 1012, triggered, they say, by his desire to take revenge for the ethnic cleansing of Danes by the English, an event referred to as the St. Brice's Day Massacre of 1002. Sweyn's sister, Gunhilde, was killed in this massacre, and he may have been seeking revenge for her death.

In 1013, he led a full-scale invasion, and an account of the event from the *Peterborough Chronicle* tells it like this:

"Before the month of August, King Sweyn came with his fleet to Sandwich. Very quickly he went round East Anglia into the mouth of the Humber and so upward along the Trent until he came to Gainsborough. All Northumbria bowed to him, as did the people of Lindsey and the Five Boroughs. He was given hostages from the shires, some with his son, Cnut, and they went to Oxford where the town dwellers soon bowed to him and gave hostages. From there he went to Winchester and the people did the same, then eastward to London."

"London put up a strong resistance led by King Aethelred and Thorkell the Tall, the Viking leader now in allegiance to the English, so he went west to Bath, after which Aethelred surrendered and went with his sons into exile."

This final event left the throne to Sweyn, and he became the first Danish king of England. Unfortunately, he died about five weeks later, perhaps deservedly so. He is reported to have been cruel and brutal, burning women alive and impaling children on lances. But his short-lived reign and then death created extreme political instability in England and left it open to what would culminate in the Norman Conquest.

Leif Eriksson: Leif the Lucky (970-1020)

Son of Erik Thorvaldsson (Erik the Red), Leif Eriksson is credited with being the first European to make landfall in North America, nearly 500 years before Christopher Columbus. He was raised in Greenland with his two brothers, Thorvald and Thorsteinn, on an estate called Brattahlid in the Eastern Settlement. From there, he voyaged to Norway, was blown off course to the Hebrides where he spent the summer, then went on to Norway, where he accepted the mission of introducing Christianity to Greenland.

He is most noted in the *Saga of Erik the Red* and the *Saga of the Greenlanders* for his famous voyage to Vinland, the name for North America. A merchant named Bjarni Herjolfsson had sighted land to the west after also being blown off course, and later Leif traced Bjarni's trip.

"He purchased Bjarni's ship and with a crew of 35 men, the expedition was organized to set sail to the new land. He landed first at the rocky place of Helluland, the flat rock land [today's Baffin Island, Nunavut, in Northeastern Canada] and voyaged on westward to Forest Land [Labrador], and so to the luxuriantly vegetated place where there are many salmon."

He reportedly overwintered there and continued to explore, discovering many vines, giving rise to the name Vinland. He returned in the spring to Greenland with a cargo of grapes and timber.

Soon, other Vikings made their way to the new world. Thorvald Eriksson led one such expedition, and in typical Viking fashion, their encounter with the *skroelingjar*, the native people, led to hostility, violence, and bloodshed. Because of this, the history of these contacts has been lost. There was no way for the people of that time to recognize that Leif Eriksson had stumbled upon a vast new continent that would one day have global implications.

Christopher Columbus claimed to have visited Iceland in 1477, and it is very likely that this is where he heard of the new world beyond the sea. He did not set off into a void as some history would tell it.

Canute Sweinsson: Cnut the Great (985-1035)

Canute Sweinsson was a prince of Denmark, son of Swein Fork-Beard, and a king of the North Sea Empire, which included Denmark, the north of England, Norway, and parts of Sweden, which he acquired after many years of Viking activity in the region. Cnut was notorious for casually leaving hostages after cutting off their hands, ears, and noses, leaving the message that the English had broken an agreement, even though that agreement was with Swein, his father, and that since Swein was now dead, they were released from their bargain.

After battling with the English for over a year, most of which was with Aethelred and his son, Edmund Ironside, they eventually agreed to terms. Cnut was to have the north of England, and Edmund would keep the south for his lifetime, after which it too would pass to the Danes. Within weeks, Edmund was dead, likely murdered, and Cnut became king of the whole of England for the next 19 years.

One of the benefits of having a Viking king was that he could protect England from Viking raids, which had been weakening the country for 30 years. He also married Aethelred's queen, Emma, thereby stopping any challengers from the previous dynasty, and he executed one of Aethelred's sons and forced another to take refuge in Normandy.

He is credited with harmoniously uniting chieftains of Denmark and England without using brutality or force, a tactic he employed to maintain his power over the two kingdoms. However, he was also a bigamist, having the queen Emma of Normandy in the south and another, Aelgifu of Norhampton, in the north. This did not sit well with the Catholic Church, so he began to repair all the monasteries and churches that had been damaged in Viking raids, and he restored their plundered treasures. Whether he was motivated by faith or politics, he was able to win them over and get significant concessions for his people under Popes Benedict VIII and John XIX. He also obtained reductions for tolls his people had to pay on their way to Rome.

Harald III Sigurdsson: Harald Hardrada (1015-1066)

Harald III Sigurdsson, nicknamed Harald Hardrada (hard ruler), is one of the most famed Viking leaders. Before his reign as king of Norway, he took part in the Battle of Stiklestad at the age of 15 with his half-brother Olaf Haraldsson, who was later to become St. Olaf. Olaf was killed as the two attempted to reclaim the Norwegian throne, which Cnut Sveinsson had taken two years earlier, and Harald was wounded and went into exile, eventually landing in Russia. He and his Viking contingent were welcomed as mercenaries and were soon employed as protectors of the emperor. Harald rose to commander of the elite Varangian Guard and soon found he had celebrity status.

His reputation now preceded him. The Guard was ordered to man the Byzantine warships, and Harald took his men into the Caliphate, where they took eighty Arab strongholds, and then to Jerusalem, where the whole country was given to him.

When he returned to Constantinople, he was accused of holding onto gold that rightfully belonged to the emperor and was subsequently thrown into a dungeon.

"Shortly, a woman with two servants came and let down a rope into the dungeon, allowing Harald and his men to escape. They went forthwith to the palace and killed the guards, seizing the emperor to put out his eyes and castrate him."

Once again, Harald returned to Scandinavia and began raiding the coast of Denmark, where the illegitimate son of Olaf, Magnus the Good, was now king. Magnus was unwilling to fight his uncle, and they agreed to share the throne. Conveniently, Magnus was dead a few months later, leaving Harald the sole ruler. In 1066, now virtually a career warmonger, he was killed at the Battle of Stamford Bridge by Harold Godwinson, the new English king. He was perhaps the last of the great Vikings.

Chapter 8

The End of the Viking Era

"Viking" is a word for which there is no substitute, no synonym. This word alone is the only one that really encompasses the broad category of people, their activities, and the events that took place in the 8th to 11th centuries.

Through all the years, the Viking Age is vivid in the memories of many, including our modern history, but history is fluid. It changes over time as our perspective changes, and as new information is made available to us. It would seem that the events that happened are unalterable. However, the place of the Vikings in history is relative as our values, morals, religions, and societies change, and as we evaluate things differently.

Today, the Vikings still bring into sharp focus images of a terrifying people jumping from beached longships and pillaging rural communities. Yet, surprisingly, they are still seen as larger-than-life, almost heroic people. History has shown us the reasons for this. It has justified, to some degree, their plundering rage against what they saw as the destruction of everything they stood for as a people before they were known as Vikings.

The Village of Stamford Bridge: The Last Stand of the Vikings

In September of 1066, England was ready to engage in battle on their southern coast with the Normans, who were assembling their forces across what is now the English Channel. At the other end of the country, however, a fleet of 300 Viking dragon ships was bearing down on them from the northeast, carrying 9,000 warriors.

One city after another fell before them as they lined up their ships for miles along the riverfront headed by the fierce Harald III Sigurdsson of Norway, aka Harald Hardrada, a Viking who was a practiced warlord with a career that spanned more than 35 years on the battlefield. His chief ally was Tostig Godwinson, the exiled brother of King Harold Godwinson. Anxious to take revenge against his brother and return to England, he found a willing conspirator in Hardrada. At the same time, the unsuspecting English awaited the Normans.

"Many of the commanders of the English armies were green, new to the battlefield. They positioned their men along the road, protected by the marshy ground on their left and the river on their right. When the battle ensued, they hacked their way against each other, shields clashing and blood spewing, fighting for every inch of ground and dying from their wounds."

"But Hardrada proved a battle-hardened foe and his military strategy quickly gained momentum against the English. He swung his troops away from the river and forced his opponents into the marsh, where many were drowned or killed by the point of a blade. The marshy flow became halted by the blood and bodies of the English."

"And so it was that the Viking contingent settled on Stamford Bridge to receive their bounty; the hostages, cattle and other goods that were the spoils of war. The Viking leader left his camp with a light group of men and encamped in the meadows near the bridge."

Meanwhile, about one week before the Vikings invaded from the north, the other King Harold, who had been awaiting the Normans, sent the citizen militia back to their shires and had dismissed the housecarls. Housecarls were what we might call mercenaries or professional soldiers. When he was told about the battle up north, he quickly changed his tack and reassembled his forces to several thousand strong.

As he neared the area, he received word that Hardrada and his men were camped within 10 miles of their position. Now he planned to take them by surprise. At dawn, 25 September 1066, the army departed for Stamford Bridge.

Hardrada's army was indeed taken by surprise. They had accepted their victory and were unprepared for another attack. Having removed their heavy hauberks, they lolled by the river near what is today Battle Flats Farm.

"The Viking sentries spotted the dust rising from the road some miles away, just over the ridge, and they were expecting their spoils to be delivered. The sun flashed off Saxon armor, and they quickly realized their error. They raced to prepare for battle, sending scouts to hold back the English, but they were swiftly overtaken."

"Yet one lone Viking defender stood greater than 6 feet tall with broad shoulders and a massive battle axe ready to cut the Saxons down. In this, the Vikings were able to assemble their defense."

"But Hardrada, the berserker, was speared in the groin and the English poured over the bridge. The Norsemen walled themselves with their shields against the onslaught, and a savage and ferocious battle ensued, each man slashing savagely amid the fray. The Viking commander fell, and the fever of battle caused the warriors to circle their leader in a corpse ring, fighting in a final frenzy."

"The victorious Saxons were merciful, allowing Hardrada's young son, Olaf, to sail home free of ransom. Only 24 longships of the original 300 were needed to carry the surviving Vikings, and the bleached bones of the dead littered the fields of Stamford Bridge for 100 years."

The French, however, led by Duke William II, later styled as William the Conqueror, had been raping the countryside in the south, and the Saxons received little rest as they rode to muster a defense. However, they were weary, and the outcome was not a victorious one for the English. Ironically, many Vikings had pledged their allegiance to the French crown, and Normandy had been under Viking control since 911, so many of the Normans who came from the south to invade England in 1066 were probably of Viking descent.

It is not clear when the Viking Age officially ended. As with much of history, there was no one definitive moment or event that ended this period. Magnus Bare-Legs, who had become king of Norway, died in a raid in Ulster in 1103, but Viking raids in Wales continued into the 12th century. The Hebrides were still under Norwegian rule until 1266, Orkney until 1468, and Shetland until 1469.

The Battle of Stamford Bridge is considered to be one of England's most significant military victories, and it marked the last time a mostly Scandinavian force would assault the island nation. After centuries of bloodshed and terror, what we think of as the Viking

Age, which lasted more than 300 years, was at its end.

By this time, the Vikings had more or less converted to Christianity. All the Scandinavian kingdoms were Christian, and the entire culture had begun to change.

Today, signs of the Viking legacy can be found mostly in the Scandinavian origins of the language in England, Scotland, Ireland, and Russia, and in the names of the areas where they made settlements. However, the lore of the Norsemen has been left behind. As strange as some of their beliefs were, the richness of the culture should be remembered for what it was: one of exploration, war, creativity, and inspiration.

Chapter 9

Norse Myths from Facts

There is no evidence, either historical or archaeological, to support many of the myths created about the Norsemen. Much of their depiction may have come from the imaginations of artists who were inspired by the ancient Greeks and Romans or by the romantic, heroic images of them portrayed in modern movies.

1. The Vikings did not wear horned or winged helmets.

Norse, Celt, and Germanic priests wore horned helmets for ceremonial and ritualistic purposes, and writers such as Plutarch mention northern warriors in horned and winged helmets, but that was several hundred years earlier, long before the Viking Age. Bronze Age (2500-800 BCE) and Iron Age (1200-550 BCE) helmets have been unearthed, which have horns. However, Viking battle helmets were typically bowl-shaped and later bullet-shaped with nose and cheek guards, and in some cases, were ornamented with carvings.

2. There were no women Viking warriors that we know of.

There were famous women, usually the wives of Viking warriors or Viking kings, who played some part in the development of their history, either by marrying into or across dynasties, killing their royal husbands, or supporting the cause of Christianity, but the image of the female Viking warrior with chain mail skirt and armored breastplate wearing a horned or winged helmet is not supported by history.

3. Most Vikings were not buried in their boats.

Viking boat burials were not common. This honor was reserved for the most valiant warriors and raiders, and for prominent people, including free women of high status. It was believed that the vessels that served these people in life would carry them into the afterlife and serve them there. They were surrounded by weapons, goods, sacrificed slaves and animals such as horses, oxen, and dogs. Even if they were cremated (burned), they were still sent off with their weapons and valuable goods for the afterlife. Many artifacts unearthed from Viking burial sites include knives, axes, swords, ornate cups, drinking horns, pottery, and other items. Although, in many cases, they are now covered with rust, X-rays have shown them to be in extraordinary condition.

4. Norsemen were not farmers.

In the true sense of the word, any Norseman who was a Viking was a pirate, not a farmer. However, most of the men and women who lived in Viking Age settlements or communities were farmers. They were, therefore, not actual Viking pirates or warriors. The few hundred men from each village who went "viking" did so either part of the year or became part of the elite group who spent many months of the year raiding and exploring. These were career Vikings, some of whom became mercenaries.

5. Women had rights.

A free woman could inherit property, get a refund on her dowry if a marriage did not work out, and could request a divorce. She could own thralls (slaves), have her own money, and generally marry whomever she chose when she was as young as 12 years old.

6. Vikings were slave traders.

As part of their plunder, Vikings would often take women and young men from Anglo-Saxon, Celtic, and Slavic settlements, which they would then sell at large slave markets across Europe and the Middle East.

7. Norse culture had standards for hygiene.

It is a little hard to understand how these men could drive an axe through an enemy's head, yet create laws that forbade them to throw dirt on someone to disgrace him, but that was what the *Grágás* (medieval Icelandic law book) stated. Severe penalties were inflicted on those who made someone dirty by pushing him into water or urine or food or dirt if the intent was to disgrace that person.

Archeologists have discovered wooden combs, metal tweezers, picks of bone, ivory or antler thought to be used to clean the teeth, and scrapers that would fit into the ear and so are thought to be ear cleaners. Items like these have been found at virtually every site that contained the remains of a body, whether male or female, and the conclusion is that they were commonly used in all Viking societies.

"Combed and washed, every thoughtful man should be, to ride to the Assembly though he may not be very well dressed; and fed in the morning, for one should not rush headlong before one's fate."

Hot spring baths built in the Norse era are still in existence today in modern Iceland, and a treaty negotiated in 907 between the Byzantine Empire and the Norse people of Sweden who traded with them stated that the Byzantines were obliged to provide them with baths as often as they wanted them.

8. People died younger in those days.

Many skeletal remains show people living into old age, up to 80 or more years, though they succumbed to joint degeneration, failing eyes, and loss of hearing, the same old age maladies we suffer today. What differs, however, is that they did not suffer from diseases of stress, though one would think the battlefield to be the most stressful place. Even warriors lived and fought well into their fifties if they managed to avoid the axe before that.

Chapter 10

Norse Mythology and Modern Culture

Though hundreds of years have passed since the writing of Beowulf, it is still a famous story that reflects all the heroic qualities we expect from an epic adventure. He risks his own life with courage and resolve to save others. He is as fearless as any modern-day hero who meets the challenges of his fate bravely, knowing that the memory of his deeds will live on.

Trilogy of the Ring

Much of the tales of *The Hobbit* and the *Trilogy of the Ring* (*Lord of the Rings*) was taken from ancient stories of Germanic, English, and Norse origin, including the dragon and his treasure, ancient runic writings (of dwarfish tongue written in elvish script) and giants (orcs, goblins, trolls, and the Balrog). Tolkien ingeniously fashioned his tales of middle earth around Midgard, where humans dwelled, and set them in the Middle Ages, the period in which the Viking Age took place. Even the ship which carried the elves to their homeland in *The Return of the King* was modeled after Viking ships, and the swamp through which Frodo and Samwise must travel on their way to Mordor resembles the swamp at the mouth of Grendel's cave as described in *Beowulf*.

Tolkien interwove many of the dark moods and texture of Viking and Anglo-Saxon poetry into his work. He was an Oxford academic who specialized in early Germanic literature, poetry and mythology, and in philology, which deals with the structure and relationship of languages. The influence of ancient Norse mythology in *Lord of the Rings* is evident.

As a boy, he read and translated the Old Norse language and the *Elder Edda* (*The Poetic Edda*), and these were a profound force in his work. It is well known that he derived the names of the dwarves in *The Hobbit* from the first of the poems in the *Edda*, the *Völuspá* (*The Prophecy of the Sibyl*).

"I don't much approve of The Hobbit myself, preferring my own mythology…to this rabble of Eddaic-named dwarves out of Völuspá, newfangled hobbits and gollums invented in an idle hour, and Anglo-Saxon runes." (J.R.R. Tolkien)

Although Tolkien took much of his material from the Old Icelandic literature, his work is not to be taken as a direct translation of the facts, but as an entertaining fabrication that mixes language, history, details, and myth into a creative interpretation of medieval times.

Pre-Christian and Post-Christian Germanic Themes and Religion

There are numerous examples of merging narratives among Christianity and Teutonic or non-Celtic traditional beliefs, with many subliminal constructs that inform Christianity as well as the concept of a democratic society.

The tales of Norse mythology reveal the belief that all the awe, splendor, and horror of the sacred was in everything that lives. They witnessed the visible cycles of the sun and moon and all the things that repeated themselves throughout their days and nights. These phenomena were perceived as being divine, and all the stories and tales handed down through the generations were backed by the belief that everything was holy.

Their worldview was comprised of the images they saw daily rather than our modern-day collective history, as seen through books and media. They held an animistic view where everything was spirit; everything had consciousness; everything had a will. They believed that if they could "see" or "perceive" something, it could also see or perceive them, and that included animals, trees, plants, stars, and everything else in their world. Everything was part of the big picture, the same narrative, the same story of life unfolding as it should. Their lives were their stories.

Men tried to live in harmony with the gods. The tribes of gods and men celebrated their victories and mourned their losses. They were deeply intertwined, and often the gods were in disagreement with each other. Different gods had different sets of values, unlike the monotheistic religions of today.

The Origin of Truth

Today we know that man has a reasoning mind that sets him apart from the rest of the animal kingdom. We process information and think logically. "I think, therefore I am." (Descartes) Modern man assumes some truths to be self-evident, but this cannot be the case - or there would be no debate, no conjecture, no questioning regarding how thought originates.

In Odin's tale *Mead of Poetry*, it is told that extraordinary insight and bursts of overwhelming brilliance, the kind of creativity and genius that is most rare, come from Odin, the highest of the gods. This is seen as a gift that could be manifested only over the drinking of mead, which induced a sort of ecstasy. This was a ritual during which one could become closer to Odin himself. Anyone could align himself or herself to the truth in this way, contrary to what the Greeks believed – that these moments were reserved only for the elite in the hierarchical social structure. Many Greek philosophers, including Aristotle, believed that inspired thought should be replaced by rationalization, analysis, questions, and logical proof. However, as we know, there was never any "proof" to be had, and there still is no proof regarding the origin of thought and the entity we call god. All knowledge is subjective and personal, originating from a particular reality between people and their worlds. As our worlds change, so does our knowledge and truth.

Themes
There are many differences between the pre-Christian, Norse or Germanic philosophies and the worldview of modern culture, with prevailing themes.

Animism
This was the belief that every living this has consciousness and a living spirit, and is not reserved to the brain in any species, in contrast to the belief that the human brain holds consciousness.

Pantheism
Germanic religion held that gods were part of the existing world rather than residing in a "heaven" or "hell" exclusively.

Polytheism

The Norse believed in many gods and goddesses rather than one divine being.

Shamanism

This was the belief that reality could be perceived during a state of ecstasy induced by mead, something many still believe, but which is frowned upon in modern society.

Totemism

They believed there was no separation between humans and everything else in nature. Man was part of nature and all its cycles as opposed to the modern belief that humans are "individuals" with souls that set them apart.

Wyrd (Urd)

This was the concept of destiny or fate, as seen through the belief in Yggdrasil, the Tree of Life, which draws life from the Well of Urd. The water cycle returns from the tree as dew and expresses time in a circular, not linear, passage. The belief was that the present could return to the past and alter it in some way, allowing humans to "work out" their karma, so to speak. Essentially, the present could be worked out through the past, and the past could be changed by the present in a cycle which is continual. Unlike the Greeks, whose fates were immutable, Norse fates, although carved into the tree by the Norns, could be rewritten.

Thaumaturgy

A fancy word for magic; Germanic culture held that if their will was strong enough, their fate could be changed through the use of magic.

The pagans believed in an afterlife, one which was determined by their fate and their actions on Earth. While the Old Testament Christian Bible does not support this, the New Testament does. One possible reason is that there was a strong need to convert pagans to Christianity, and adopting some of their beliefs was helpful in accomplishing this. In this way, Western European culture thrived and spread.

- The One God replaced Odin, and all the other gods were allowed to be worshipped as intermediaries.
- The death of the god Baldur, Odin's son, and his return or "resurrection" were seen in the death and resurrection of Jesus.

- Easter is so-called after the Germanic goddess Eostra.
- Odin pierced himself with a spear and hung on Yggdrasil so that he could attain spiritual knowledge. In the same way, Jesus, as one and the same God and the Son of God, sacrificed himself to himself.

"I know that I hung on a windy tree, nine long nights, wounded with a spear, dedicated to Odin, myself to myself, on that tree of which no man knows from where its roots run." (*Havamal*, st. 138, *Runatal* (*Odin's Rune Song*))

- Priests who now ruled over temples and shrines (formerly held in individual homes) were accepted as a type of kingly office.
- So how else does Old Norse culture influence modern society?
- The names of the days of the week
- Festivals, which began as shared worship, are now held around a particular theme

Christmas, called Jul in Scandinavian countries, is a more secular event and is celebrated around:

- The yule log: A large block of wood that was burned to signal in a new year, later incorporated into the Christmas celebration and burned for 12 days, but not burned completely.
- Holly: As with any animistic religion, English Holly held the Holly King. Its berries were bright red in winter and seen as a type of magic, so bringing holly boughs into the home was believed to give a place for good fairies to linger, keeping away evil. The holly should not be kept up after the 12th night, however.
- Mistletoe: The famous story of the death of Baldur, son of Odin and Frigga, is that he was killed by a mistletoe spear by some trick of Loki. Upon hearing of her son's death, Frigga wept, and her tears turned to the white berries of the mistletoe. She placed the mistletoe on Baldur's chest, and he returned to life. Today, mistletoe is seen as a symbol of love and is praised for its curative powers.
- Exchange of gifts: There are many stories about why we exchange gifts at Christmas. Odin exchanged one of his eyes for wisdom from the guardian of the well. However, in general, the exchange of gifts was an expression of love, trust, and cooperation.

Films and Comics

Ancient heathen worldviews have also extended into modern culture through a host of media in movies and comic books, with socio-cultural effects that have influenced how people perceive and interact with their world. They represent the themes of heroism, the battle between good and evil, fate or karma, man's will against the universe, and man's frailties or vulnerabilities. However, one may be surprised to know that, although Norse mythology is used to some extent, the original stories were changed in large part due to the ethics and morality of the time.

When Stan Lee and Jack Kirby wrote the Marvel comics universe in 1962, they had to eliminate all the blood and gore, the murder and sex, from their magazines because they just would not be publishable if they kept true to actual Norse or Viking events, whether mythical or real. But despite Hollywood and Marvel's changes in the legends and tales of the gods of old, these modern-day interpretations serve to inspire curiosity about a culture that lasted more than 1000 years.

"Do you swear to cast aside your selfish ambition and pledge yourself only to the good of the realms?"
"I so swear."

"And on this day, I, Odin, All-Father, will proclaim you."

Thor

Thor, a son of Odin and god of thunder or weather, is one of the most popularized characters. His hammer and belt offer him great strength, but their magic is endowed by Odin, showing us that we are obliged to a force greater than ourselves. In the Marvel version, a blonde Thor must "go beyond the sacrifice of Odin." He is sent to Earth, where he learns humility and love before he is allowed to go back to Asgard.

Thor did not speak with a British accent. In fact, Norsemen did not speak English at all. Thor was not blonde, but redheaded. He did not marry Jane, a human. He married the goddess Sif, and he was not banished to Earth to walk as a human.

Loki

Marvel has changed Loki into an evil-doer instead of the mischief-maker he was in the original tales. But some of the tales of Loki – for example, his tying his testicles to a goat to make the giantess Skaldi laugh – would never have made it into either the comics or the movies.

Sif

The goddess Sif was the goddess of the harvest, not the warring slaughterer portrayed by Marvel.

Odin

Marvel's Odin is portrayed as a peace-loving father who banishes Thor in the movie of the same name for starting a fight. However, the real Odin, the god of war, went looking for it.

Frost Giants

The frost giants were not evil trolls. The real frost giants are the Jotuns who grew out of Ymir's armpits and who were supposed to be very wise.

Conclusion

Norse mythology is larger-than-life, filled with sagas of warriors and kings who made fighting a career, of gods and goddesses who were also human, and of a world divided among the gods and giants who began the world.

Their achievements, vibrant culture, and craftsmanship have significantly contributed to our world today, and their explorations helped make up the boundaries of nations. They warred with the Franks, England, and Ireland, and traded and explored as far as the Muslim and Byzantine Empires, and into Russia, Spain, and North America. They came from Sweden, Norway, Iceland, and Denmark, and defended their tribes against the onslaught of Christendom.

They traveled rivers and seas easily in longboats able to go where conventional vessels could not, and they were able to navigate waters without benefit of the sun to guide them. They lived and died in the name of Odin, god of the battle-slain, and their history continues to enthrall us today. Modern translations may not do justice to their battles and honor. However, their stories are told with great magnificence, with all the enthusiasm of the splendid sagas.

Bibliography

The Völsunga Saga. Trans. Eirikr Magnusson and William M. Morris. London, Stockholm, New York: Noroena Society/Harvard College Library, 1906

Beowulf. Unknown. Circa 700-1000

The Prose Edda. Sturluson, Snorre. Trans. Rasmus B. Anderson, LL.D. Chicago: Scott, Foresman and Company, 1901

The Prose Edda. Sturluson, Snorre. Trans. Brodeur, Arthur Gilchrist, Ph.D. London: Oxford University Press, 1916

Konungs Skuggsjá. Unknown. Trans. Laurence Marcellus Larson. New York: The American Scandinavian Foundation, 1917

Historia Norwegiæ. Anonymous. Trans. Peter Fisher. Copenhagen: Museum Tusculanum Press, 2003

Landnámabók. Unknown. Trans. Herman Pálsson and Paul Edwards. Canada: University of Manitoba Press, 2007

Annals of Ulster. Unknown. Trans. Sean Mac Airt and Gearoid Mac Niocaill. Dublin: Dublin Institute for Advanced Studies, 1983

Heimskringla. Sturleson, Snorri. Trans. Samuel Laing. London: Norœna Society, 1907

Orkneyinga Saga. Unknown. Trans. Jon Hjaltalin and Gilbert Goudie. Edinburgh: Edmonston & Douglas, 1873

A History of the Viking Age. Carlson, Robert. 2015

Vikings: History & Mythology. Weaver, Stephan. 2015

J.R.R. Tolkien: A Biographical Sketch. Doughan, David, The Tolkien Society, 2014

Made in the USA
Coppell, TX
04 June 2020

26895519R00058